Kaleidoscope

artistic techniques for the creative soul

elisabeth keely wilson

KALEIDOSCOPE: Artistic Techniques For The Creative Soul

Copyright © 2000 by Elisabeth Keely Wilson

Brookside Press, 111 Brookside Place, Danville, California 94526.

Library of Congress Cataloging-in-Publication Data

Wilson, Elisabeth Keely
      Kaleidoscope; Artistic Techniques For The Creative Soul/
    Elisabeth Keely Wilson.
          p.   cm.
      Includes bibliographic references.
      ISBN 0-9701038-0-8
        1. Creativity-Techniques   2. Intuitive Painting-Techniques
    3. Spirituality   4. Meditation   5. Visualization

    00-190928   2000

First printing, 2000

Printed in Korea

Dedicated to the three "men" in my life :

my husband, Greg
and our sons,
Gregory and Bradley

Preface

Seen as a metaphor for life, a kaleidoscope illustrates the truth of beauty emerging out of the midst of chaos. From the outside, the bits of colored glass and beads of a kaleidoscope seem to tumble together somewhat meaninglessly, without any apparent shape or form. One must look through the lens—from a different perspective—to see the beautiful patterns emerge.

On the surface, our life experiences might be likened to that jumble of colored chips—having no apparent meaning, no particular form. However, if we can pause for just a moment and step back, thereby gaining a new perspective, we are presented with a colorful mandala pattern, a clear reflection of the wisdom and beauty of the creative life force.

This book contains many moments of reflection: moments when the images in my mind were joined with my own inner wisdom and were brought forth through pen and paint. When creating, I move and breathe from a place that encompasses my whole being—my body, my mind, and my spirit. The results of my creation I consider a gift of nature—a gift for allowing myself to be open to the healing power within and also for my willingness to move and flow with a presence which I cannot see.

My gift in return is the sharing of these experiences, with detailed descriptions of the various methods and techniques used, so that you too might journey beyond your everyday existence, guided by the creative spirit that lies within each of us. With the willingness to explore unknown territory, you will discover that same wellspring of creativity from which you may draw, reflecting the beauty of your own true nature in its expressive form.

A creative journey of self-discovery . . .

Contents

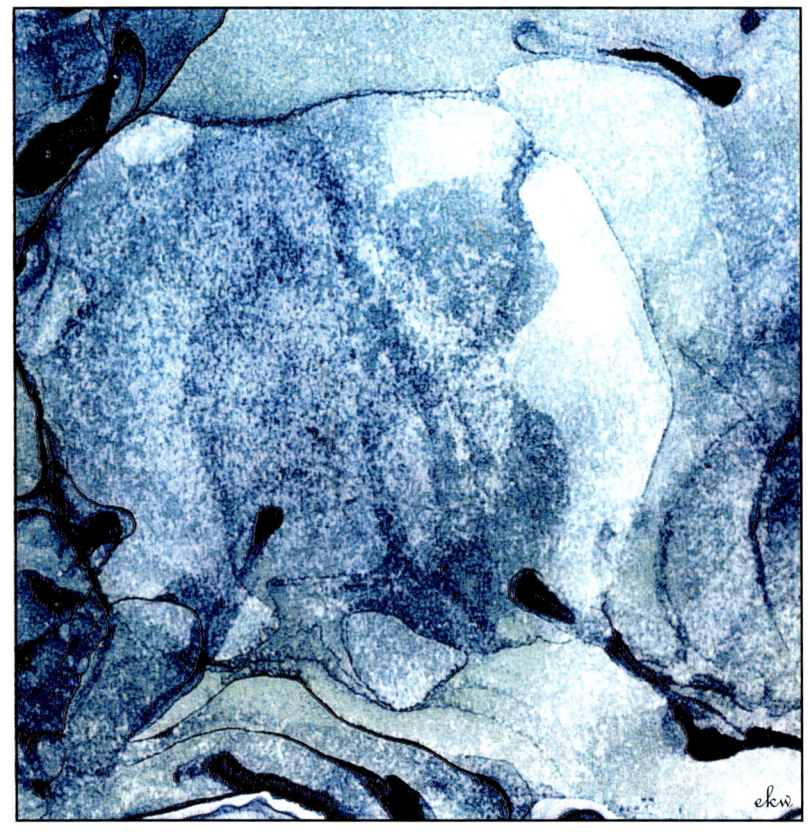

. . . is an inner quest toward wholeness.

Contents

The heart awakens
a single moment at a time,
a single step at a time.

How This Book Came To Be

no longer who i believed i was
i know not who i might become . . .

These words, written several years ago, prefaced my own inward journey as I discovered a "place of grace" where I came to know myself once again—not as a writer, as a designer, as a mother—but simply as a being. The beauty and wonder I discovered over the course of my inner exploration is reflected within the pages of *Kaleidoscope*, illustrating the trail of my footprints. Each painting, each piece of writing, reflects one brief moment of awareness, one small step on the long journey back towards my self.

By opening the heart to the creative spirit that resides within, anyone—artist or non-artist—can access that inner source of creativity, expressing one's true nature through symbolic visual imagery. Beginning with the tools of intuitive art—paper, paint, and water—all that is needed is the willingness to step into unknown territory and to honor the wisdom of the inner self. Responding, at an instinctual level, to the elements of the painting process allows for beautiful impressions to develop that are, in essence, a gift of nature.

While the intuitive process is based on entering the unknown, there is comfort in recognizing the direction in which one is headed. With this in mind, details of the various methods and techniques used to create the paintings in *Kaleidoscope* are woven throughout the book and are presented in greater depth within the Appendix. Just as each person has a signature that is uniquely his or her own, each of us has a unique way of combining the elements of our world through visual expression. My experience, as reflected in *Kaleidoscope*, is offered simply as a starting point, from which you, the reader, might discover your own reflections of the creative life force.

The beauty within your eyes is a reflection
of the beauty within your heart.

How To Use This Book

Kaleidoscope presents a series of poetic reflections mirroring the beauty and wisdom of the source of life, illuminating the mystery of the unknown, revealing a path of self-discovery through the creative process, and portraying the deep trust and connection to the soul that exists within each of us.

The quest to know one's true nature is both a creative journey and a spiritual journey, inspired by an inner impulse toward wholeness. To enter the creative process is to be willing to be a little lost—lost within the depths of the unknown and the mystery that is life. Yet it is within the act of embracing the unknown that true growth and healing occur. Bravely stepping into unfamiliar territory, we release the hold of old beliefs and judgments, thereby opening the heart to the wisdom, creativity, and insight that have always been there, deep and true.

Experienced as a whole, in sections, a page at a time, or again and again, *Kaleidoscope* offers a way of perceiving and being that awakens the body, the mind, and the spirit through the practice of meditation, visualization, writing-to-write, and intuitive painting. My hope is that you will use this book as a reference point—for your own exploration and creation, and more importantly, for your own discovery of the beauty that lies within. Just start wherever you are, fully present and awake, and allow yourself to experience the joy and wonder of dancing in the light of the spirit.

ekv

*Allow yourself the gift of experiencing
the completeness of life.*

Each Moment . . .

each moment that i . . .

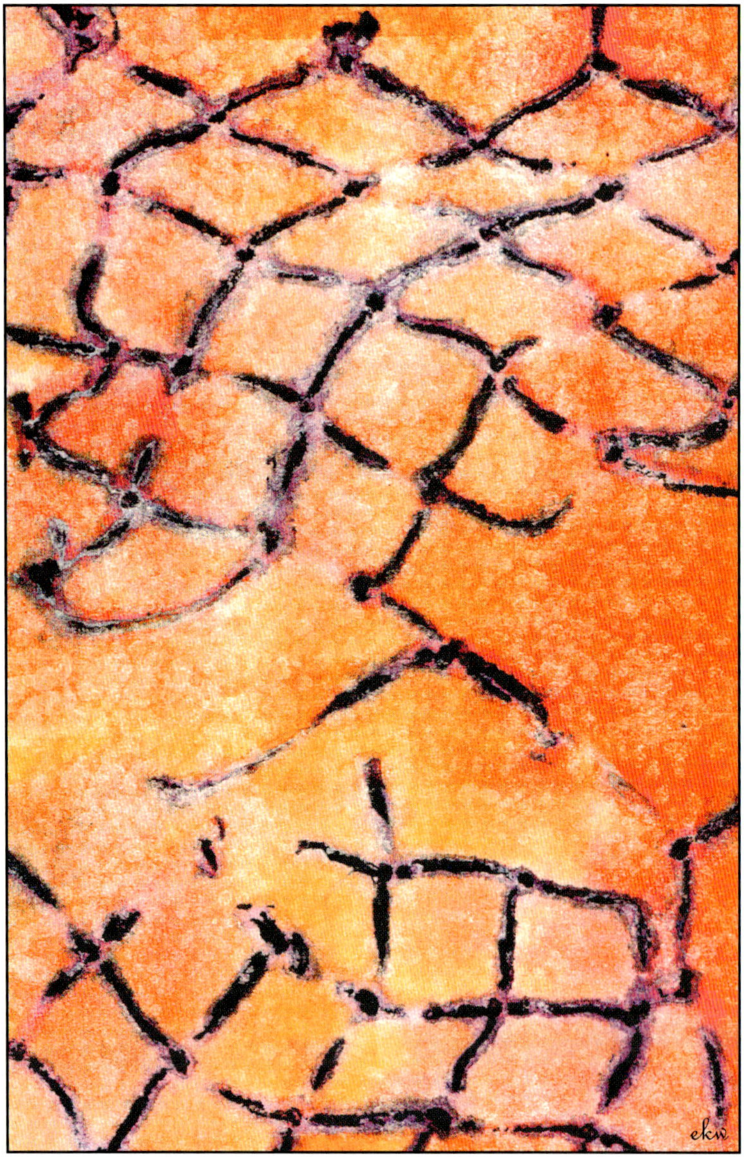

Oh, sweet release!

Sweet Release

Gave myself a gift—
the sweet release from being
who i ought to be,
was schooled to be,
ever yearned to be.

Opened myself to the
breadth of the moment—
discovered a state of grace,
nothing more was required / needed,
i was enough to simply be.

The purpose of life is to be—
as a leaf, as a rainbow, as a being.

In This Moment

Every drop of rain, every petal of a delicate rose, holds the truth of the beauty and mystery of life. When I can be still and witness the miracle of the ordinary, I open myself to a world of wonder.

To live in a sacred manner is to honor that which is right before me in each moment, making any moment that goes by unnoticed, a lost gift.

A solitary leaf softly whispers my name, inviting me to stop and discover the world through childlike eyes.

To know the beauty of the rose is to carry that beauty within. Resonating with the harmony of nature's grace, I am filled with gratitude for the gift of awareness.

The simple act of being places me on a path toward my true self. Stepping into the silence, I am poised on the edge—between the dance of life and the stillness of being. In this moment, all sense of time and timelessness disappears. This is the only moment there is.

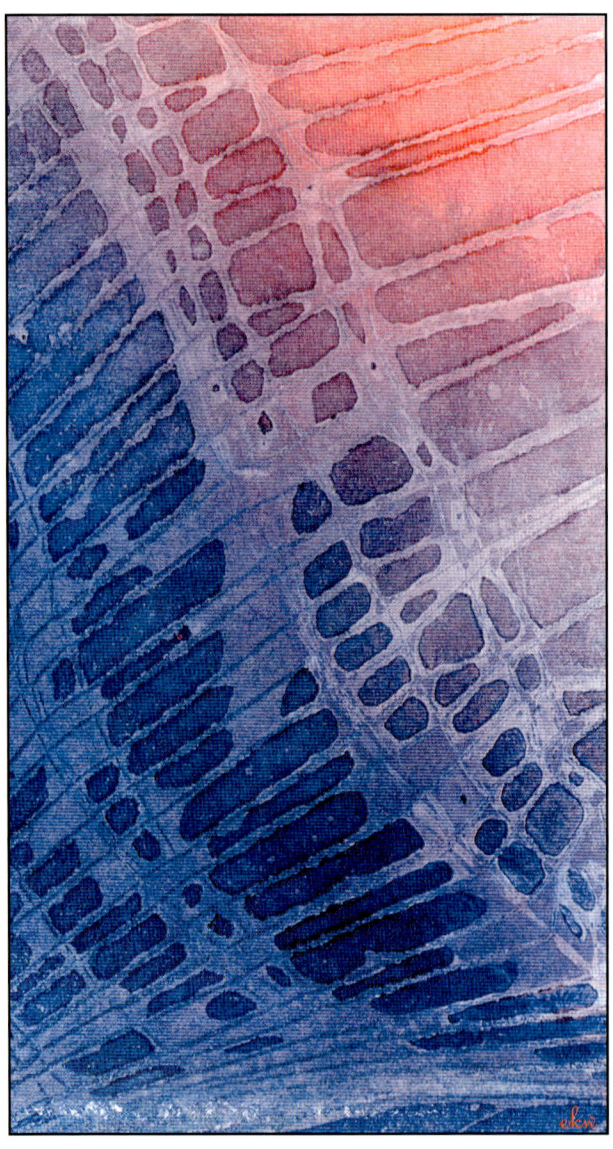

*Life is a tapestry of sunlight and darkness,
chaos and beauty.*

Essence Of Life

The thread of life weaves its beautiful tapestry, winding sunlight and darkness, beauty and chaos, reflecting a sense of myself woven into the delicate fabric of being.

♦

We are all ordinary human beings, blessed with the gift of life, able to touch the divine spark within us in a single moment of awareness.

♦

The seasons of the heart can be wild or calm, benevolent or destructive; all aspects of living are inevitable on any journey of awakening.

♦

It is the simple things—the touch of a loved one's hand, the vibrant glow of the evening sky, the sweet smell of raindrops on a gust of wind—that touch the willing heart.

♦

Reaching beyond the concept of the self as an individual, the interwoven nature of reality brings with it a sense of self that is shared by all. I, too, am a part of the whole.

♦

The essence of life is where I begin and where I end. It lives within me, it lives within you. It is the beginning and the end.

♦

Stillness is the window to the soul.

Stillness

The path of my journey will be revealed to me, moment by moment, if I can be still and listen to the silence.

◆

Stillness is the beginning of movement just as darkness is the source of light. Deep within the shadows surrounding my heart, I see tiny sparks of brilliance among the darkened embers, reassuring me that I do have the strength and courage to take the first step.

◆

In the still of the moment, I touch my tender heart—that connection between my own life and the divine. It is within this soft spot that I find my sanctuary—a sacred space where I am free to grow, to heal, to be.

◆

On the gentle wings of a mourning dove, I am lifted out of my own confusion.

◆

Honoring the gift of silence, any sense of separation between myself and the whole disappears. I am you. You are me. We are one and the same. I am.

◆

A journey of awakening begins with the breath.

Center

When I turn within myself, I remember all that I have forgotten while I was so busy looking outside myself for the answers to life's unanswerable questions—therein lies the light of awareness.

My breath resides at the center of my being. Following the path of the breath as it moves throughout my body, my senses gradually open to the fullness of the moment.

Working from the center of myself, I move outward toward the world.

If ever I should lose my footing, I know the way home is as close as my breath.

Focusing on my breath, I allow any physical sensations, feelings, and thoughts to simply come and go. With practice, I become a witness to my own self, recognizing that I am not my thoughts and feelings— they simply flow through me as a stream winding its way through a mountain glen.

*In that moment of silence,
open your heart and you will know love.*

An Open Heart

To live a life of integrity is to surrender to the natural wisdom of the creative life force.

◆

Opening up to the mystery of myself, I am asked to enter the unknown and to follow my instincts. Hidden within the cloud of unknowingness resides a presence which is constantly guiding me toward my true self.

◆

With the willingness of my tender heart, I awaken the healing energy that has always been there, deep within me, bringing light to the darkened recesses of my mind.

◆

To walk a path of the heart is to gently hold both sides of the self—the faulty and the divine, the flawed and the flawless—embracing all aspects of myself with compassion and love.

◆

Accepting the complexity of life, I become aware of the presence of exquisite beauty in a world of tragic suffering.

◆

hello, hello

Hello

today
for the first time
caught a glimpse of self
not yours
not theirs
mine

deeply buried
beneath a mound of rotting compost
infinite possibilities to behold
encompassing all that is
nothing more
nothing less

my self
hello

Visualization Exercise
Opening Your Heart

To live with an open heart is to move toward the self, to be able to hold your own hand. The intention of opening your heart acts as a seed which is planted in the soil of the spirit. Whatever choices and actions follow will support and nourish the growth of that seed.

Sitting in a straight-back chair with your feet on the floor, close your eyes and inhale deeply. As you exhale, notice your breath as it moves throughout your body. Inhale deeply again and then exhale. Now breathing naturally, bring your attention to the top of your head. Exhale as you gently let your attention move downward toward the tip of your toes, checking for areas of tension or tightness. You can soften these areas by breathing light or warmth into them with your next breath.

When you feel comfortable, move your attention to the area of your heart. Gently holding your heart in your mind's eye, notice its softness as well as its sturdiness. Imagine your heart gradually opening to the light within you, just as the blossom of a flower might open its face to the morning sun. Rest quietly within this openness, letting its warmth and glow flow over you and through you. As you sit with your open heart, you may become aware of bits of fear and resistance that arise—just know that these feelings will come and they will go. The warmth within your heart will remain strong and true.

Before opening your eyes, repeat silently to yourself, "My intention is to live with an open heart." Anytime during the day, if you find yourself feeling anxious or somewhat lost, ask yourself this question—what is my intention? While answering yourself silently, "My intention is to live with an open heart," let the image of your open heart appear within your mind's eye. Notice how your entire body softens and feels lighter. This is walking a path of the heart.

Meditation Practice
Back To The Breath

Meditation is used to strengthen the connection between the inner self and the outer world. Focusing the attention on the breath, meditation provides a point of repose for self-discovery—allowing one to open what is closed and to explore what is hidden.

It is best to meditate in a location that is sheltered from noise and has a minimum of distractions. Allow yourself ten or fifteen minutes to sit quietly, resting in the center of your breath. There is nothing else that you need to do, nowhere that you need to go. The world, in all its wonderful complexity, will manage without you and will still be there when you return.

Letting your mind rest in the breath, notice the experience of the physical sensation of air as it travels throughout your body. How does it feel inside your nose, as it goes down your throat? Is it cool? Is it hot? Opening all your senses, pay attention to the taste and texture of the breath as it moves upward and moves downward. Just be with the breath and watch it flow.

If any thoughts or concerns come to mind, acknowledge them as thoughts, and then gently bring your attention back to your breath. Practicing the art of non-attachment allows you to let any thoughts or feelings you might have just float by. For this brief period, you have given yourself permission to simply be at peace in the light of the world.

If you find yourself wondering whether you are meditating correctly or not, you needn't be concerned. Meditation practice is just that—practice—there is no right way or wrong way to meditate. There is only you sitting quietly within the soft embrace of yourself.

Part II

You are a beautiful star child
shining your truth through the mist.

Each Moment . . .

each moment that i—

    see the world through childlike eyes . . .

*You have all the strength and courage
you will ever need.*

Unknown Journey

no longer who i
believed i was
i know not
who i might become.

bravely stepping into the unknown
my footsteps are illuminated
by an inner strength and wisdom—
this journey is my own.

Your childlike innocence is ever present.
It is within this pure innocence
that your true nature lies.

Creativity

Upon seeking a path to explore one's inner nature, creativity offers itself as a doorway leading to the landscape of the soul.

Born of openness and innocence, creativity explores with the curiosity of a child. To follow the muse of my childself is to listen to the soft voice within and to trust in my perceptions.

A creative journey is a spiritual journey. Through spontaneous creative expression, I bring the inner world of the spirit together with the outer world of the waking self.

Embodying all aspects of the world—creativity reflects the fullness of life within its ebb and flow—the light and the dark, the known and the unknown.

Creation is about meeting myself wherever I am. I start where I am and come to know and accept myself exactly as I am—body, mind, and spirit.

Creativity doesn't happen to me—rather, it flows through me.

Go out and greet the world
with open arms.

Imagination

Imagination lives in uncharted territory. It is one's willingness to honor the inner self that sheds light where there once was none.

The light of my imagination moves through the many layers of my being—exposing all illusion of darkness—illuminating the inner reaches of my heart.

Imagination, as the expression of its creator, flows through every piece of work, no matter the medium, technique, or style, bestowing bits of brilliance to brighten the world.

The outward expression of one's inner images is the touchstone for inner transformation. The process itself acts as a "container," allowing for the release of thoughts and images held from the past, thereby creating space within the mind and the heart for new perspectives and untold possibilities.

Imagination is the sister of transformation—side by side, the two make the impossible become possible.

The angels celebrated the day you were born.
Be with the angels and rejoice in who you are.

Child's Play

In a child's mind, the imaginary is real and the real is imaginary. There are no boundaries, no limits. Anything and everything is possible.

◆

The spirit invites me to be childlike and to play. I'm not sure I know how. As I made my way in the outer world, with its many masks and roles, I lost touch with my playfulness.

◆

The greatest muse of all is my childself. It is the source of my inspiration and my creativity if I am listening. When I stop and welcome the silence within, I am inviting the muse to show herself.

◆

Connecting with the curiosity and spirit of my childself, I create for the pure pleasure of beautiful chaos—suddenly, I remember how it feels to play, to be silly, to make messes.

◆

When I create, I feel as if I am playing. Creating simply for the process itself, rather than for any specific outcome, releases my thinking mind from its critical stance. Working from my center, I enter the realm of self-discovery with the innocence and wonder of a child.

◆

Your presence on this earth
brings light to all whom you touch.

Writing-To-Write

The practice of writing brings me back to the beginning—to the part of my mind where daffodils rain and the cow jumps over the moon. This part of my mind is full of energy and passion and is not concerned with goals or outcomes.

I write simply for the act of writing—letting go of all expectations, I am free to write whatever comes. I write without stopping, exploring the landscape of my mind, being a witness to my thoughts as they come and go.

The purpose of writing is to move beyond my thinking mind and reach the wisdom of my inner self. As I write, I become aware of dropping deeper into my self, going down through the layers—down, down—finally reaching what I know to be my inner truth.

Writing is a path to opening my mind and my heart, to becoming my own best friend, to learning to trust my instincts.

Writing gives me practice in accepting myself exactly as I am.

You are a star child
shining your own ray of starlight.

It Is What It Is

Poetry has a mind of its own—it likes to arrive unexpectedly.

A point of repose—poetry is a refuge where there is no right or wrong, no good or bad. There is only what is. It is a sanctuary, where I can speak my truth without fear.

The images, sensations, thoughts, and feelings flowing through me are joined together and echoed in the written word—leaving behind a stream of crystallized impressions floating through space and time.

As the voice of reason, poetry erupts spontaneously, always telling the truth.

Presented with "poetic license" I am given the liberty to eloquently express my thoughts and feelings through the beauty of the written word, without regard for conventional form, logic, or fact.

*The sacred thread of life connects the
spider to the sky as the blossom to the moon.*

Geography Lessons

the source of human nature
resides deeply beneath
the web of love and pain
drawn to the point of stillness
i am touched by the
whisper of a butterfly
as it delicately stretches
its newly formed wings

time and space merge with love and betrayal
as new life grows within me
at once i am student and teacher
illustrating the truth
that i hold the entire world within my being
in all its essence
its beauty, its love
its reach for the truth

Visualization Exercise
Discovering Your Inner Sanctuary

Either sitting or lying down, let your body and mind soften as you begin to watch your breath. Resting in the breath, imagine yourself moving across a bridge that connects the outer world of the self with the inner world of the spirit. On the other side of the bridge lies a trail for you to follow as you let all the thoughts and worries from the day float away. This is the only moment there is.

You find yourself walking toward a place that feels safe and secure, a place where you can be at peace with yourself and your world. It might be anywhere—a sandy cove edged with softly lapping waves, a mountain peak capped with snow, a favorite hideaway from childhood. The setting of your sanctuary is relevant only to you and you may find it frequently changes because you are constantly changing. What doesn't change about one's inner sanctuary is the underlying sense of being held, protected, and loved within this space.

After reaching this safe place, look around and you will notice an old wooden rocker that is just your size. The chair seems to be beckoning you to sit. Upon taking your seat, you gradually become aware of the sensation of warmth originating deep in your belly and spreading throughout your entire body. You are in your inner sanctuary—a place that is for you alone—to be at one with the world.

Rest quietly within this spot for whatever length of time seems necessary. When you feel complete, slowly retrace your steps, gradually moving your awareness through your body toward the bridge of consciousness. As you step off the bridge, you open your eyes, ready to join the world.

Writing Practice
Writing From Within

Writing practice is sacred time, spent within a sacred place. It is a time when there are no rules to follow, no judgments to be made. There is only you, sitting quietly, with your writing hand moving across the pages of your notebook as the words flow from a source deep within you. You write whatever comes to mind—without stopping—for a block of time that has been carved out of your day or week, expressly for the practice of writing.

Before you begin, close your eyes for a few moments, allowing your awareness to gently drift—away from the busyness and concerns of the everyday world—toward a place of solitude and calm within you. Imagine your senses opening to the many sights and sounds you may encounter along your inward journey. Upon reaching that point of refuge, open your eyes and begin writing. Write whatever comes to mind, without stopping to think about it—just write.

This is a time when you need not be concerned with punctuation or spelling or if your paper looks messy. It is the writing process itself that is of importance as you explore your inner landscape, discovering aspects of yourself that have previously been hidden or forgotten. If, at any point, you become aware of the presence of your inner editor, thank it for its input and then send it on its way. While you may want to edit what you have written at a later date, the present moment is reserved for free expression, without constraints.

Continue writing, expressing your innermost thoughts and feelings, until you have the sense that there is nothing more you need to say. Before bringing your awareness back to the outer world, stop for a moment to close your eyes. Center yourself in the breath, and thank yourself for giving yourself the gift of your attention.

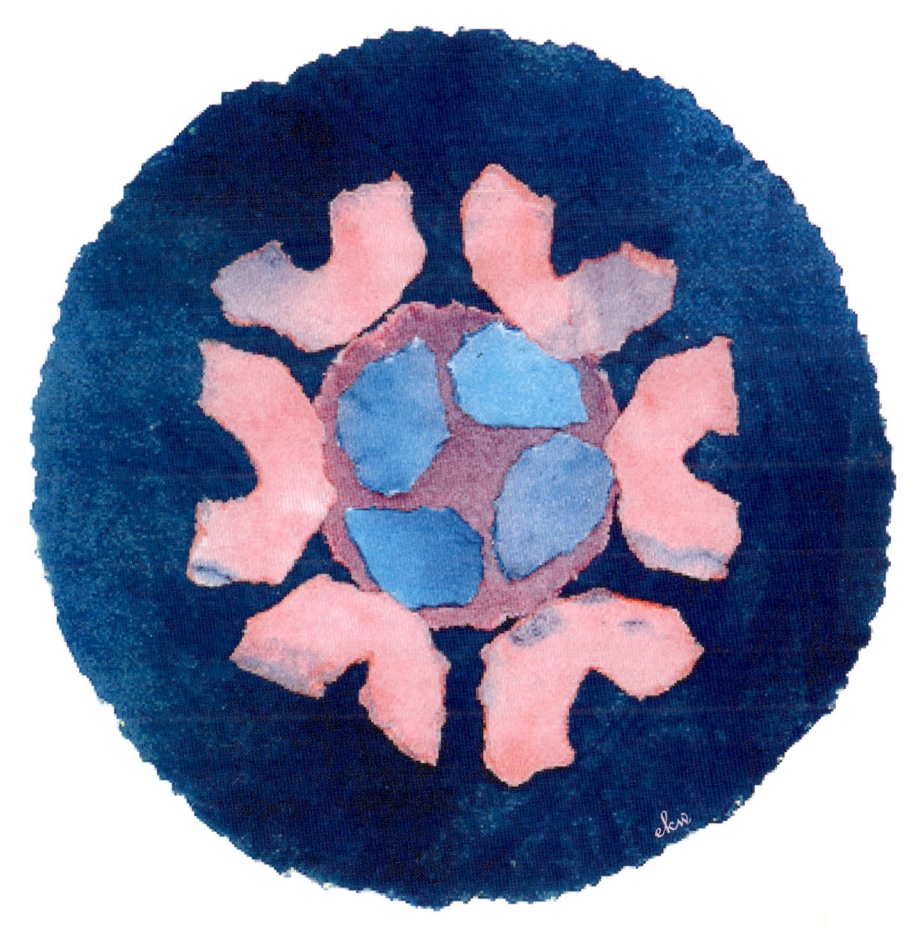

You are not the past nor are you the future.
You exist only in this moment.

Each Moment . . .

each moment that i—

    see the world through childlike eyes,

    listen in silence
        without the distraction of inherited voices . . .

Deep within your heart lie the answers you seek.

My Identity

i found my identity tucked in his handsome billfold
nestled between a tattered photo of our
two blue-eyed boys and his blue cross insurance card
filed there many years before
personally insured with a hefty deposit
all for security's sake—but who is security?   at what price?

in a moment of silence
caught a whisper of myself
its echo reverberated to the depths of my soul
that account which i deemed so very safe and secure
now bears a cryptic message upon its steely face
"account closed—long overdue"

perhaps the time has come
to open an account
under the terms of my own intrinsic value
a sign in the window states
"beautiful handmade satchel offered to anyone opening
a new account previously held by an outside owner"

my identity i will place within its soft confines
near a newly captured image of the three "men" in my life
encased by a self-portrait
painted to the rhythm of my heart
~
not for security's sake—for my own sake

Paint with the angels!

Of Art And Angels

A delicate lace impression appears on the stone entrance of an ancient church in Mexico. The intricate and beautiful pattern speaks eloquently of art and angels.

◆

Long, long ago, local villagers decided that the dark and dreary space at the front of the church needed to be made more welcoming. After attempting to paint the walls but not satisfied with their efforts, the locals gave up in frustration and went home to pray. Upon their return to the church the following morning, the villagers found that their prayers had been answered! An exquisite lace pattern now graced the once bare walls. It had to be the work of the angels!

◆

It was later discovered that lace, dripping with paint, had been placed upon the wall by one of the locals, only to be quickly forgotten. By morning, the pieces of dried fabric had fallen to the ground leaving behind a delicate, ethereal effect which was promptly attributed to the angels. Let the angels paint!

◆

Be still and find yourself in the silence.

Intuitive Art

The soul longs to create just as the plant craves the sun and the sun reflects the moon. When I bring forth the beauty that lies within me through the experience of painting, I give myself the chance to witness the beauty of the soul.

Images and impressions that I hold within the landscape of my inner self heal and replenish me, providing me with a point of refuge from the complexities of the world. Using creative artistic techniques, the images within my mind can be joined with my own inner wisdom and brought forth through paint and paper.

The intuitive process offers me a world of possibilities—all that is needed is the willingness to allow myself to be guided by curiosity, to be willing to step into the unknown. With willingness comes a view of the world from a different perspective—life is no longer seen as simply black and white—instead I am surrounded by a kaleidoscope of color, shape, and line with which to discover and to create.

The ability to create beauty is a birthright and lives within each of us. Reaching beyond old attitudes and beliefs I may have held about myself, the creative process taps into my deeper knowing, releasing the artistic sense that has always been there.

Listen to the forest to find your path—
your strength and courage will light the way.

Coloring Outside The Lines

Speaking through color and texture, shape and line, intuitive art acts as the "container" bearing the essentials of experience. Beginning with the very simple tools of paper, paint, and water, I am instantly encouraged to color outside the lines—to do what comes naturally from within myself rather than from what has been learned or studied.

◆

It takes an open mind and courage to step into the unknown. As I face the white expanse, I am asked to step into that void and to explore with nature. Paying attention to the subtle responses I feel from within, I am guided as to what the next step will be.

◆

I become a co-creator with nature by turning within myself and following my own inner guidance as to the specific colors to use, the movements to make. Intuitive art is not concerned with the use of any specific artistic technique; rather, it invokes the painter to become a part of the whole, to be at one with nature, in the process of discovery and exploration.

◆

Holding to my inner truth, I am carried by the spirit of nature to new levels of discovery and understanding. Trusting in the wisdom of the self, I find that as the color moves and flows, so too, do I. As I learn to follow the movement of the colors, I become more aware of the ever-present spirit within me and its guiding force in all areas of my life.

◆

*Your greatest challenge lies in
embracing the unknown.*

Expectations

The ancient truths run as a river beneath the surface of my life—
I become aware of their influence as I reach more deeply within
myself throughout the creative act. As the process itself becomes
the teacher and I become the student, I am a witness to the wisdom
of simplicity, patience, and acceptance, as reflected in the artistic
flow.

It is here that I get to practice accepting life on life's terms.
Intuitive art manifests a paradox of life—I want to control yet I am
not in control. As I complete my part of the painting process,
guided by my inner knowing, I am aware that I must let go of the
outcome—the spirit of nature will make the final determination as
to the texture and even the true colors of the finished piece.

The completeness of the painting process depends upon my level of
playfulness, my desire to discover, and my willingness to be guided.
Allowing myself to become one with the painting, I am presented
with beautiful impressions that seem, in essence, to be a gift of
nature.

Letting go of the belief that the true meaning of life is found in
understanding its complexity, I become aware of the gift of
simplicity as I am shown the beauty of the world from within.

Forgiveness opens the heart
for love to bloom.

Inner Healing

When life gives you pain, embrace your sorrow. When life offers you joy, celebrate your happiness. Greet each moment's grace with open arms and a tender heart.

◆

The inner experience of intuitive painting is the foundation for living in the present moment. Once the connection is established, something very deep inside opens, allowing healing to occur— old sorrows are released, new perceptions are discovered, a deeper connection to the self is created.

◆

Ghostly images of the past can darken my thinking when I deny or resist their presence. I become aware of their influence through the outward expression of my emotions. When I don't judge my feelings, I can be fully aware, thereby releasing the shadows of the past in the present moment.

◆

As I learn to trust in the wholeness of my true self, the wound within me softens, healing in its own space and time. The inner healing is reflected in each piece of work—within its forms, images and color— this is the gift that is taking place upon the inner landscape of my psyche.

◆

The wounds of the past are
released in the present moment.

Cry Me A River

recovered from a wasteland
of outer desolation
my hardened heart
was gently wrapped in loving kindness
and placed on the hearth
of compassion's door

this heart of mine
cracked open wide at the first sign of softness
and sorrow flowed
like a river
high above its banks
spilling tears for my child self

cry me a river
cry until there are no more tears
cry, little one, cry
cry until you are empty
cry
just cry

Visualization Exercise
Color Me . . .

Sitting quietly with your eyes closed, allow your awareness to rest on the movement of your breath. Following your breath as it flows upward and downward, bring your attention to any areas of tightness or tension, letting those areas soften with the next exhalation. As you continue breathing, gradually become aware of a heavy, warm, safe sensation surrounding your body. Allow yourself to sink into this heavy warmth as any last bits of resistance or worry float away. Rest assured that this time is a sacred time, and that all is well.

When you feel ready, let your attention sharpen and your inner witness become more observant. You may notice that the flow of your breath isn't simply a physical sensation or an invisible presence; it has taken on its own color and shape. Now, you can clearly see your breath as it moves throughout your body, spreading and blending its beautiful essence. Continue breathing as you open your senses to the fullest, letting your awareness be enveloped by this precious giver of life.

Before moving your attention back to the outer world, sit within the wonder and beauty that is you, recognizing that this beauty can be expressed in the world of your waking self. Your breath, which is the basis for life as you know it, is the link between the inner world and the outer world. The more you come to know the breath, the closer you are to being at one with your true self. Know, as you move once again toward the waking world, that your breath is always there— wherever you go, there it is.

Painting Beauty
Going With The Flow

Arrange your painting supplies on a table. Sitting or standing, take a moment to center yourself—closing your eyes, bring your attention away from everyday matters toward your inner self. Let your awareness rest in the breath as you silently state the intention to honor your intuition by expressing your inner beauty. Focus on your breathing, with or without your eyes closed, until you feel connected to that deep place of inner knowing. Begin when you feel ready.

Attach a full sheet of paper to a sheet of foam board or plywood using masking tape. With a wet sponge, gently wash water over the entire paper. As the paper begins to dry, use a squirt bottle to apply squirts or drips or drops of paint to your paper, letting yourself play with the paint and the water. Pick up the board your paper is attached to and tilt it from side to side, noticing the effect gravity has on the movement of the flow. As the paint spreads, leaving shades of color in its wake, let your intuition guide you as to what to do next— to add more water or possibly another color.

If you feel uncertain at any point, step back and take a breath. Let yourself rest within this space, allowing the pleasure of completely being in the moment fill your senses. When you feel an inner tug or have a clear thought as to the next step, go back to your painting. Once you believe that you have fully expressed yourself, cover the entire piece with plastic wrap, letting the wrap fall however it may. On top of this, place a sheet of plywood. Now it is nature's turn to play.

Let twenty-four hours pass before removing the plywood. After making sure the paint is dry, carefully remove the plastic wrap. Beyond your own application of color, nature's imprint upon your work is now revealed. Through the painting experience and the practice of patience, you have been given a gift of nature—the beauty and wonder of your own inner landscape.

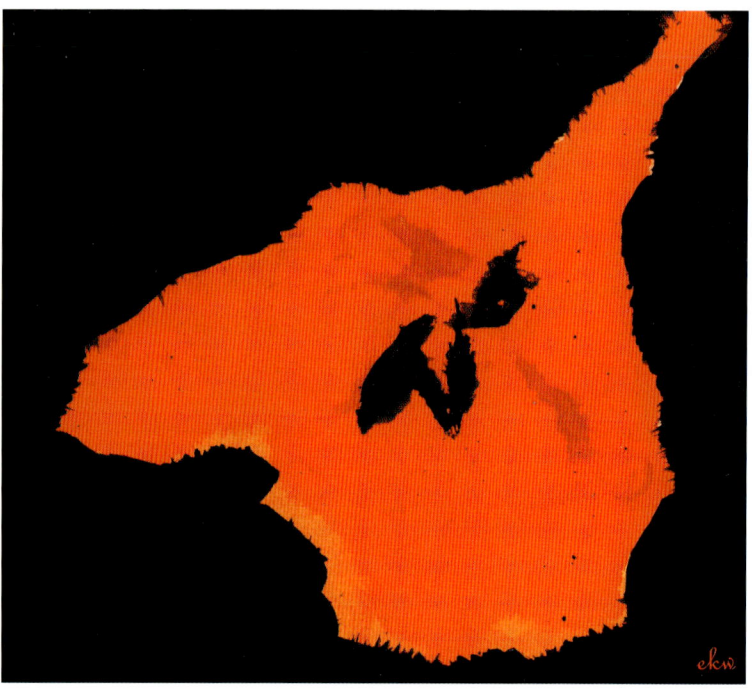

Part IV

The divine spark within you is the
embodiment of your true nature.

Each Moment . . .

each moment that i—

    see the world through childlike eyes,

    listen in silence
        without the distraction of inherited voices,

    speak what i know to be true for myself . . .

The spirit of nature encompasses all that is.

Nature's Own

pretty as a picture
a picture is worth a thousand words
need anything more be said ?
seductively conditioned
beauty stands tall
a testament to one's personal value
a statement of societal worth

a flash of clarity
illuminates
the distant reaches of my mind
this beauty, so desired
is an illusion
a cleverly designed mask
compromising Nature's own

to be pretty as a picture
is to live an untruth
look, but don't touch
the image might shatter
breaking into a thousand tiny pieces
thereby exposing the jagged terrain
just beneath the surface of my life

*To trust one's intuition is to
walk a path of wisdom.*

Trusting My Intuition

Intuition employs the language of the heart—a language based on feeling, rather than on logic. I allow my feelings to be free in the present moment as the act of creation flows. Reaching deep inside my being, I express the truest part of myself.

◆

Trusting my intuition as the inner authority, the experience of painting takes on a life of its own. Opening my awareness to the unexpected, I sense what is needed from moment to moment—responding only to what is.

◆

Paying attention to the sensory details surrounding me, I become increasingly aware of my bodily responses to life—a quickening of my heartbeat, a catch in my breath, a gentle flip-flop in my belly.

◆

Witnessing the wisdom of the painting process deepens my trust in the presence of the creative spark within me. The finished piece authenticates this trust—thereby strengthening the sacred thread connecting the spirit to the self.

◆

With practice, the awareness of my intuitive sense begins to extend beyond the creative process, linking my waking self to my inner knowing as I move throughout the day. As the separation between my inner world and outer world softens, life, in and of itself, becomes a spiritual practice.

◆

Compassion is the doorway
to inner transformation.

Nature's Gift

Each of us is given the gift of choice. Having the power to choose, I have the power to bring change into my life. I can change my mind. I can choose once again.

Change rules our lives and our hearts. Some moments will be open and warm; others will be dark and difficult. Each moment will come and each moment will go. This is the basic law of impermanence.

It is my resistance to change that causes me to suffer—not change itself. When I can meet my resistance with a heart of compassion, I open the door to the possibility of transformation.

There is comfort in knowing that nothing in life is permanent—everything is in a constant state of motion—this is as true for the stars in the midnight sky as for the frogs croaking their nightly lullaby.

Practicing the art of "going with the flow" through the painting process, I become more adept at accepting change in all areas of my life. When I find myself in a place of resistance, simply by accessing the wisdom of my inner artist and recalling the sensation of the flow of paint, my body yields, allowing me to join the current of life.

Your courage flows through you—
strong and sure.

Daring Not To Know

Creativity, in its purest form, recognizes that the essence of beauty is found in following one's own truth, wherever that leads.

◆

Fear is a natural response when moving toward the truth. Without fear, there would be no need for courage.

◆

When I can embrace my fear as a friend who has much to share, I become aware of an underlying sense of strength and courage flowing through me—I am enough for this world.

◆

Letting go of what I think I know, the energy of the unknown rises within me. My challenge is to remain open to the sensation as it moves through me like a mountain spring—silently running over, around, and through any obstacles along its way.

◆

Intuitive art offers itself as a sanctuary where there is nothing to fear—there is no right or wrong—no good or bad. There is only the creator, in hand with nature, speaking the language of the heart.

◆

*May the beauty within you
sing and shout.*

A Voice Of My Own

Painting is a way to begin again—to know who I am, what I think, what I know, what I don't know—the words can be added later, but first, I have to paint.

Beneath the layer of conscious thought lies the source of my unique self—a self that speaks in the language of feelings and symbols. I discover my inner truth through the painting experience, as colors flow, forms and shapes emerge, and content reveals its beauty.

As my voice grows stronger, the images, thoughts, and feelings within me merge, creating a singular trail for body, mind, and spirit to resonate as one.

Expressing my truth—my heartache, my pain, my joy—brings forth shadowy images long forgotten or denied. By spontaneously painting these unresolved feelings, I open myself to the healing power of nature's grace.

Forgiveness is the doorway through which true healing lies. As I remember and release the sorrows of the past, I stand on the threshold of the present moment with a generous heart and the warm embrace of compassion—not only for myself but for all beings.

Transformation begins in the heart.

To Hear, To See, To Speak

hear no evil
see no evil
speak no evil
powerful tenets by which to survive
a childhood defined
in the name of the father, the son, and the holy family

through the eyes of awareness
recognized the tragedy of a life unlived
shattering the mirror
did not destroy the image
exposed a wealth of possibilities
revealing the face of transformation

every piece contains the whole
every seed holds the promise of good and evil
every moment invites a choice
i choose to hear
i choose to see
i choose to speak

Visualization Exercise
Moving Toward The Light

Sitting in a comfortable position, close your eyes and gently let your mind wander. Take several deep breaths, blowing away the uncertainties of life with each exhalation. Gradually allow your breath to resume its natural pattern as you release any last bits of tension or tightness from within your body.

Imagine yourself standing at the top of a circular staircase that leads from your mind's eye down through your body toward the inner recesses of your self. Follow the curve of the staircase, letting it guide you, one step at a time, into the unknown. As you reach the bottom of the staircase, you find yourself surrounded by a landscape of incredible beauty and peace, flooding your senses with warmth.

Looking around, you notice a stream of light shining brightly in the distance. The light seems to be moving in your direction. You slowly walk toward the brightness, somehow aware that the essence you are approaching is your own healing energy. Your sense of inner peace grows as the distance between you and the light lessens. Upon reaching the center of the landscape, you and the white light join together and become as one.

Filled with a deep sense of security, allow yourself to remain within this healing light for whatever period of time feels necessary. When you are ready to move back toward the outer world, know that this healing presence will be with you—it is always with you, whether you are aware of it or not. If, at some point, you find that you have lost touch with that inner presence, simply close your eyes for a moment and let the image of that peaceful scene rise up and fill your senses. Simply by having the intention to stay in contact with your inner world, the essence of your inner healer can be brought to light, every moment of every day.

Painting Heart
Start Where You Are

Take whatever time you need to quiet your body and your mind. As you let the details of the day fall away, open your senses to the world directly around you. See the shape and texture of the table before you, notice the colors of your painting supplies, become aware of the placement of your body in space. Gradually move your attention from the outer world to the inner world, giving yourself ample time to establish the connection to your intuitive self.

The act of creation begins once you notice whatever feeling is present in your body in the moment. As the feeling rises into fullness, let your inner observer take in the details of its essence. Standing within the center of the feeling, watch for any spontaneous images to arise within your mind's eye. Notice if a certain image or color makes your heart beat faster or your belly jump. This is where you start.

Using a variety of materials, you can translate your feeling into a poetic visual statement. To begin, attach a piece of illustration board to a backing of Plexiglas, brush the painting surface lightly with water, and pour, spray or drip the color(s) that portray your feeling. Pick up the board and tilt it back and forth to manipulate the flow of paint until you are satisfied with the basic composition.

Now, cut pieces of recycled items such as bubble wrap, waxed paper, or cellophane, into shapes or forms that express the essence of your feeling. For instance, to represent fear, you might cut out shapes that are reminiscent of flames in order to create the illusion of fire. Place the cutouts in the wet paint, adding additional paint if needed. Cover the entire piece with plastic wrap and a heavy board to ensure contact between the plastic and the paint. Let nature weave her magic for the next twenty-four hours. When the painting is completely dry, carefully remove the plastic wrap and the cutout shapes. The images left behind are the full expression of your feeling as interpreted by nature.

Part V

The path toward wholeness is found in having
reverence for all living things.

Each Moment . . .

each moment that i—

see the world through childlike eyes,

listen in silence
        without the distraction of inherited voices,

speak what i know to be true for myself,

walk my chosen path to a rhythm of my own . . .

Between the known and the unknown
is the moment of choice.

Decisions

poised on the precipice of life
to move forward is to step into the abyss
uncharted territory
will i plunge to my death?
a sparrow broken by her own daring
or will i fall upwards on the tail of a breeze
to a world of completeness
a world of possibilities
a world of wholeness within myself?

the decision is mine alone—what choose i?

to move back from the ledge
is to remove myself from my self
a familiar place to reside
offering safety but no color, no light, no texture
only bleak emptiness peppered with fear
not life in her fullness
not really life at all
yet the lure of that place beckons me still

the decision is mine alone—what choose i?

*The breath of life weaves its essence
into the very fabric of our being.*

Simply A Journey

Be gentle with yourself. Life is not a race nor a test—simply a journey to be repeated again and again and again.

◆

In a simple moment of awareness, life itself becomes the teacher and I become the student. When I can fully accept that life is dictated by its own sense of direction and there are no set instructions—the path of my journey becomes a moment by moment discovery.

◆

Holding to the truth that this moment is all there is, I need not be concerned with what should or should not be. I am free to experience all that is before me, with the depth of my feelings providing the color and texture to life's everchanging composition.

◆

The path of following my own truth offers me new eyes with which to see beneath the black and white of life. Grabbing the threads of strength and wisdom, I weave a wrap of many colors for the long journey home.

◆

A splash of color flowing across the page is an invitation to be joyful and awake—to allow the richness of the moment to live in my heart and to celebrate the breath of life.

◆

Faith asks for truth without proof.

The Cloud Of Unknowingness

Deep within the cloud of unknowingness, I find the faith to believe in a presence which I cannot see.

◆

Faith is a way of being—it is a practice of honoring my inner self—my gifts, my strengths, my spirit.

◆

When I open myself to the mystery of the unknown, which is by definition beyond comprehension, I become a witness to the natural unfolding of life. Being open to the unexpected, I find there is a rightness to all that happens, an order to all I see.

◆

The process of painting is a sacred covenant between myself and the greater whole. Respecting the mystery that is myself, I allow my heart, rather than my mind, to speak. With my intuition guiding me, the qualities of the painting are gradually revealed.

◆

As I come to know myself throughout the painting process, my need to fully comprehend the mystery of life loses its importance. Resting quietly within the strength and wisdom of that which I do not know, I discover the answers to questions I have yet to ask.

◆

Each of us is the author of
our own inner vision.

The Artistic Sense

Pure creation is the impulse of the free and uninhibited spirit we all possess.

◆

The languages of image, feeling, and instinct are distinct ties to our evolutionary heritage. Guided by my intuition during the artistic process, the imagery brought forth becomes an act of healing, integrating past with present forms of communication.

◆

Entering the unknown with curiosity and wonder goes hand in hand with opening all of my senses to the experience before me. Trusting my natural instincts, I discover and explore my authentic responses to the world as seen through childlike eyes.

◆

For a child, there is no separation between the intention to draw a house and the actual rendering of the marks. I can honor that childlike wisdom when working intuitively by allowing myself the freedom to express "I want to do this" and "I will do this" in the very same breath—in the very same movement.

◆

The artistic process encourages the imaginary to become real and the real to become imaginary. As a form of communication, intuitive art is not dependent upon recognizable forms or symbols. Rather it speaks through instinctive artistic principles—focus, composition, color, value, and texture—to tell its story.

◆

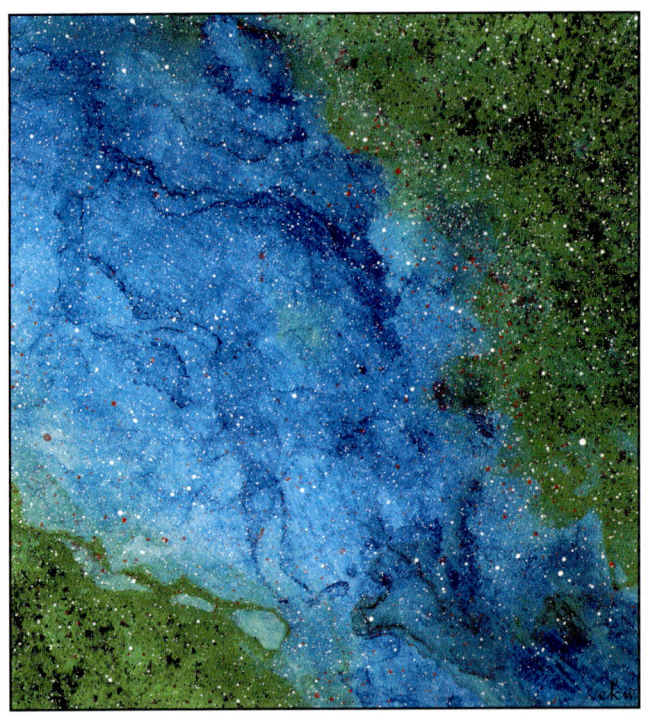

To own one's imperfections
is to make peace with the self.

Good Enough

Releasing myself from the need and the desire for perfection, a clearer sense of self begins to flower and bloom. Standing solidly within myself—rather than on the edges of my being hidden behind one of my many masks—I am who I am, not who I think I should be.

◆

To be good enough is to allow myself to be exactly as I am—secure in the knowledge that there is nothing about me that needs to be changed or fixed.

◆

Moving beyond the boundaries of my outer self, I reach beneath the black and white of life. With a heart of compassion, I can hold both sides of the opposites within myself, without rejecting the presence of either one. I witness the beauty surrounding my sorrow. I savor the bitterness within my joy.

◆

Letting go of any attachment to being special, I am asked to accept my place as one among many. Embracing my interconnectedness to others, I discover a sense of belonging, a sense of intimacy, a sense of being at home wherever I am.

◆

As I practice the art of patience during the painting process, I am reminded that all things unfold in their own time. Just as it takes time to grow a garden, it takes time for beauty to evolve—therein lies the seed of wisdom.

◆

The gift of clarity is a world of color.

Tapestry

The gift of clarity reaches beneath the mask of fear.
Unraveling the tangled threads of my origins,
i see its beauty dissolving before my eyes.
Stripping away the illusion of perfection
takes perseverance and blind trust.
This portrait of my heritage,
so proud and serene,
was preserved for eternity, protected at all cost.
Every delicate strand within its intricate structure
offered a glorious glimpse
of a glorious past—

Alas, it was only a dream.
With eyes wide open,
a riot of color and texture now lies before me.
Nature's rainbow swirls and swoons
as once again its magic weaves.
A pattern emerges embracing
all that has been denied or disallowed.
The soft underbelly of life is reflected within its misty hues,
as the silken threads of light and dark
intertwine amidst the ties of compassion.
Not a dream, this—this is the true state of my being.

Visualization Exercise
Meeting The Muse

Sitting quietly with your eyes closed, allow your awareness to move inward, gradually coming to rest within the breath. Focus your attention on the movement of your breath as it flows upward and downward. Take a few minutes to simply be, as you let the cares and concerns of your daily life slip away. Giving yourself this period of sacred time to be quietly present will strengthen the connection between your inner world and outer world, thereby affirming your commitment to yourself.

Once you feel centered, let your attention travel downward into the darkness until it comes to rest at the stillpoint—the point where time and timelessness become as one. Breathing deeply into the silent depths, notice the tiny sparks of brilliance shooting from out of the darkness. These sparks symbolize the transcendent energy of the inner muse—the source of pure creativity.

As you continue to breathe naturally, the sparks of light gradually join together to create a softly-glowing form that appears to be rising out of the depths of darkness—the source of your inspiration is preparing to share her essence with you. The inner muse may appear as a child, an adult, an animal, or simply a feeling—the form of your creative energy is unique to you, and may even change, as the muse is an entity of her own making.

Simply be with the muse for several minutes, letting the warmth of her energy gently flow over you and around you. You may want to ask if there is anything she would like to share with you before she goes. Thank the muse for her presence in your life and for revealing the treasure of herself. As you bring your attention back to the outer world, know that the essence of the muse will remain within your consciousness as you go about your day, sending her flashes of brilliance to guide your way.

Painting Spirit
Nature's Playground

The world of nature is the foundation of the intuitive painting process. Seeking out the wonder of the natural world with an artist's eye, begin to notice intricately designed bits of nature that might be used to create an imprint or texture within a painting. As you become familiar with the infinite variations of nature's touch, you may want to begin a small collection of natural objects—rocks, leaves, seed pods, bark, and shells, to be used and re-used during the painting process—providing inspiration as well as texture, form, and depth.

Arrange your collection of nature's gifts in front of you and then close your eyes. Take a few moments to center yourself, internally stating your intention to paint with the spirit of nature. Open your eyes and sit quietly, letting your gaze rest on the various bits of nature, until you feel an inner impulse to begin.

Pour, spray, or drip the colors that portray the essence of your inner expression, tilting the board to enhance the flow of paint. Once you are satisfied with the background composition, place various natural items into the wet paint, with the flattest side of the object facing down. The flatter the object, the better, as the impression created is the result of contact between the paint and the natural item. Apply additional color, or introduce a different color, if desired.

When you feel that the piece is complete, scrunch a large piece of plastic wrap in your hand, and then undo it. Place the crinkled wrap loosely on your artwork, carefully arranging the plastic around the bits of nature to help insure contact between paint and plastic. Use books or small items to help weigh the plastic down between the shapes. Let the painting dry completely (the drying time will depend upon the type and number of objects used) before removing the plastic wrap and the pieces of nature. Nature's gift to you is the unique expression of your own inner beauty as designed by the spirit of nature.

Part VI

Life, itself, is the journey.

Each Moment . . .

each moment that i—

    see the world through childlike eyes,

    listen in silence
        without the distraction of inherited voices,

    speak what i know to be true for myself,

    walk my chosen path to a rhythm of my own—

        i am one step closer to being all that i am.

      I am.

The petals
of your spirit
will dance in the wind.

Inner Composition

the pristine whiteness of a canvas blank
evokes a myriad of emotions
as desire dares uncertainty
to unveil its hidden face

to create in the moment
is a statement of raw courage
mirroring the footsteps of discovery
through the garden of my soul

spontaneous expression
embodying all aspects of creation
invites body, mind, and spirit
to blossom as one

Tend to your inner garden first.

The Art Of Balance

Tending my own garden first, I nurture the soil of my soul, planting seeds of loving kindness in the simplest of ways—I listen, I watch, I touch, I am present.

As I learn to listen to the voice of my heart, to identify that which is most deeply true within myself, and to embrace all that I have been given with gratitude, I open myself to the gift of serenity.

Acceptance of what lies before me in this moment—this knowing, this task, this experience—brings clarity of vision. Choosing to do only one thing at a time—while being fully aware—offers me a reference point between past and future, known and unknown.

Resting quietly within the natural rhythm between action and stillness, speaking and silence, I discover a point of repose from which to "do life." It is from this place of refuge that I am able to experience serenity while in the midst of chaos.

The painting experience allows me the opportunity to practice the art of balance as I explore the dynamics of water, paint, and paper—responding to whatever is happening in the moment—without getting caught by details, judgements, or expectations.

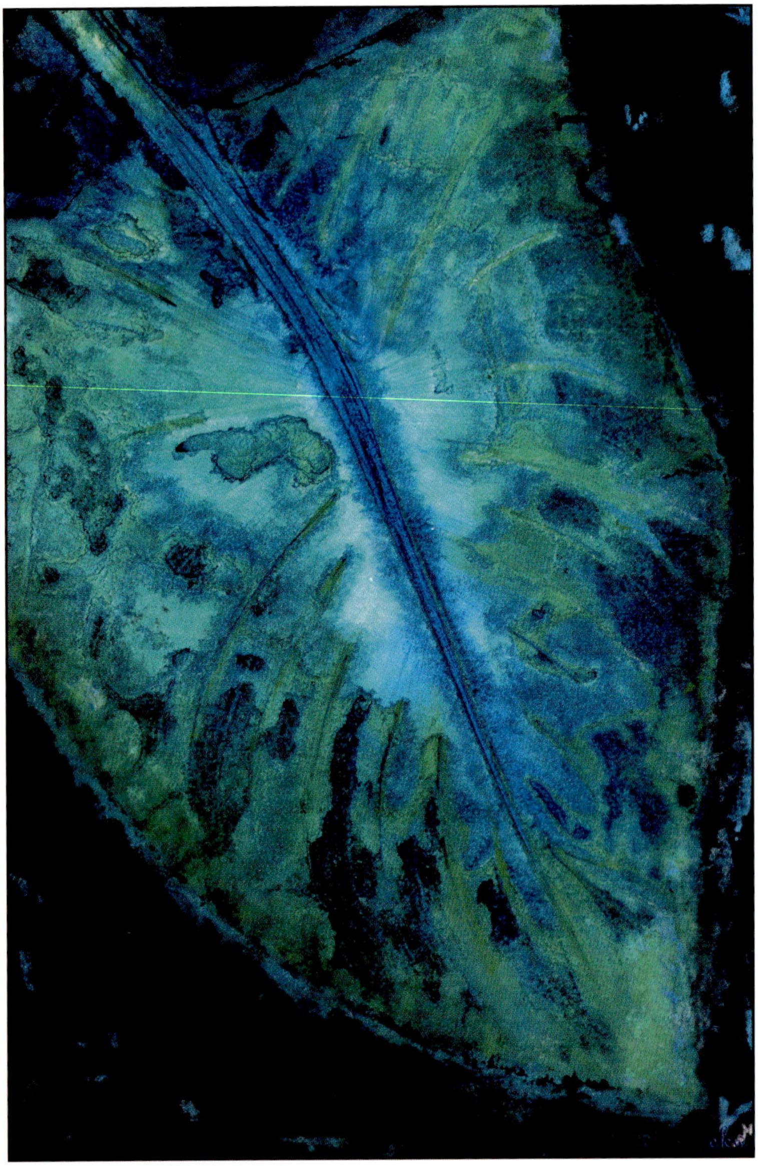

In simplicity, one finds truth.

Mindfulness

I center myself each time I become aware of what I am seeing, hearing, and feeling in this instant. I see the white paper before me, I feel the wooden chair supporting my body, I hear the wind blowing outside my window. I am present and awake.

At the heart of the painting process, a flash of color resonates with something deep and true within myself. I am suddenly filled with gratitude for the healing presence that speaks to me through the simplicity of color.

Mindfulness asks that I be conscious of what is before me in the moment. As I watch the color move across the white expanse, I open my senses to nature's grace. As the paint flows, so too, do I. Becoming one with nature, I express the part of myself that is longing to emerge.

The practice of mindfulness is built upon a foundation of trust—I learn to trust the present moment—I learn to trust myself in my willingness to be open, to observe, to reflect, to feel, to change.

The impression expressed on paper reflects the integration of myself and spirit to create—this moment is a gift of grace—honoring the timeless beauty reflected from the depths of my soul.

Above all else, to your own self be true.

Integrity

Speaking the language of the heart through pen and paint, the visible expression echoes the small, still voice of my intuitive self—connecting body, mind, and spirit as I reach deeper still.

Honoring my intention to fully experience my feelings, without withdrawing or hiding, develops a fundamental trust in my own inner resources—my wisdom, my strength, my courage—therein lies the path to wholeness.

With a courageous heart, I find that place of clarity and strength within the depths of silence. Releasing myself from the hold of past memories and future expectations, I stand poised on the threshold of a new world—a world of completeness, a world of wholeness, a world of integrity.

Integrity is a way of being—embodying my commitment to myself—to being present to the truth of the moment.

Woven into the fabric of who I am—integrity lays claim to the wisdom borne of imperfection in its search for the truth.

Beauty is found in the harmony
of the many parts that create the whole.

Whole And Complete

The only way to experience oneness is to be at one with the self.

◆

Portraying my thoughts and feelings through symbolic imagery and visual harmony, I nurture that part of myself that is ready to be born. Thus, the artistic process reveals itself as a path toward wholeness—one step at a time—one moment at a time.

◆

Throughout the painting process, the complexity of my humanness becomes more visible—each aspect of myself revealing its essence as an individual facet of a beautiful crystal. I am asked to honor all of these aspects, the light and the dark, embracing the whole of myself with compassion and love.

◆

With deep trust in the spirit of wholeness that I carry within myself, the boundaries of space and time dissolve and I experience the totality of life—the connection between myself and others, past and future.

◆

True wisdom lies in recognizing that life, in and of itself, is sacred time—making each and every moment, a moment of grace.

◆

The tree of life is
the beginning and the end.

Bare Essentials

the ancient memory
of mystery and silence
rests undisturbed within the
fragile beauty of nature's grace

stripped bare of all expectations
preconceptions
i stand straight and tall
at one with the earth

going forth in my innocence
i reach for the divine source of light
illuminating the essential me
the essential you

this is the soul of the world
this is the heart of the matter
this is all that matters
the beginning / the end

Visualization Exercise
A Path Of The Heart

Sitting comfortably, slowly let your attention come to rest in the breath. Notice the gentle movement of your breath as your daily cares and concerns gently drift away. Be aware of your breath as it moves throughout your entire body, leaving a sense of calm and ease in its wake. Breathing naturally, let your body, mind, and heart open to the fullness of the moment. This is the only moment there is.

Resting quietly, become aware of your connectedness to the earth and to the dance of life. As you mindfully explore the depths of your inner self, internally state your intention to keep an open heart to whatever rises. Honestly naming what it is you feel—your fear, your sadness, your joy—you meet yourself just as you are, with compassion and acceptance. You recognize the voice of your heart as you learn what is most true for yourself.

Now moving more deeply into your awareness, you become one with the earth as you breathe from the very center of your being. Sitting within the garden of loving kindness, you recognize that you are on a journey of the heart; you embrace what you have been given with gratitude.

Let yourself stay in this space for as long as you wish. After some time, open your eyes. To walk a path of the heart is to bring your whole heart and your whole spirit into your daily life. As you begin to move about in the everyday world, you can be aware of the state your heart is in by noticing if it feels open or closed. Each time you are able to respond to yourself with an open heart, you create one less moment of fear, one less moment of judgement. Each moment you meet yourself with loving kindness, you leave one more set of footprints on the path of your heart.

Painting Wisdom
Reflections

Each piece of artwork created in the moment is the true expression of your innermost feelings—in that moment. While the heart of intuitive painting is the artistic process itself, rather than the finished product, there is much to be learned in taking time to reflect upon the imagery of past moments and to use those expressions to build upon, in the present moment.

Saving all of the paintings that you create, finished or unfinished, gives you the ability to mine the past in the present moment. Any piece that seems unresolved or incomplete can be used again, either as a background piece or to be cut or torn as collage material. By arranging your artwork around you and letting your intuition be your guide, you will begin to notice that particular pieces are open to being developed in new ways.

Before doing any cutting or tearing, close your eyes and let yourself become centered in the breath. Thank your intuitive self for the wisdom you have received in the past and also for the guidance that is available in this very moment. When you feel connected to your deepest knowing, open your eyes and begin.

Tear or cut whatever part of the painting that seems unclear into strips or various-sized pieces. As you are tearing the pieces, let any images arise within your mind's eye. Once you feel a bodily response to a particular image, begin to arrange the pieces as if they were parts of a puzzle until you discover a composition that expresses what you want to say. Then, using an acrylic gloss medium as glue, attach the individual pieces of your design to a sheet of foam core board. If you would like the finished piece to appear as a single image, brush a coat of acrylic medium over the entire piece and let it dry. The gift of your expression is a clear reflection of nature's way—the beauty of the past is gone, only to be reborn once again.

A Fairy Tale

The Maiden And The Frog

◆ ◆ ◆

There was once upon a time a fair lassie whose very existence depended upon the heartfelt promises and sweet dreams of the most beloved of fairy tales. With a halo of golden curls and eyes of the bluest sky, this lassie answered to the name of Angelina, which according to the books of lore, meant "child of angels."

Now it came to pass that at a very early age, possibly even before the celebration of her first birthday, Angelina was told by the township's oldest maiden—truly an old maid—that all good lassies must aim for perfection each and every moment of each and every day in all acts said and done. If the lassie's efforts were honest and true, as determined by whoever it was who ruled the heavens, (it remains unclear as to just who or what that entity might be), the reward would be a pair of lovely white angelic wings with which to fly and a giant-sized portion of never-ending love.

Now being a child as she was, Angelina did indeed find it difficult to behave perfectly at all times; however, she put her best foot forward inasmuch as it came to mind. Many long days and many long nights passed as Angelina valiantly tried to reach the state of perfection so she might win the honor of waking to love's warming glow brightening her life and the sensation of feathery weightless wings upon the small of her back.

As she was quite a bright young maiden, Angelina was certain that, in time, she would most assuredly accomplish her quest—it was just taking a mite longer than she had expected. And, frankly, the whole affair was not quite the simple matter she had been led to believe. The fact of the matter was, if chance had happened by, the young lassie would have stopped at nothing to give that old maid a piece of her mind!

And so the days continued to pass as days do—the days became weeks, the weeks became months, the months became years and still nothing changed. So intense was Angelina's single-mindedness on the job at hand that she found little pleasure in the sunshine, or the birds, or the rosy clouds floating across the evening sky. To top it off, with each heroic effort on her part to enter the castle of perfection, the farther away from heaven's gate she stood. And despite the fact that the now not-so-young lassie was indeed growing weary, she persisted, for to abandon her goal would most certainly end life as she knew it.

Now no one is sure of the matter of events, but it is held to be true that one fateful day in early spring—a day like any other that began with the kiss of the sun—Angelina's world turned inside out and upside down. A solitary reference was found to have been scratched in the family album, by who knows whom. It read simply, "The demise of the small green frog was quite unexpected."

As the tale is told, Angelina's heart broke wide open when she happened upon the small, stiff body of a young frog she had recently befriended, as his life journey was her own. It quite literally took her breath away and made her heart go all aquiver, to imagine that this unfortunate little creature would not ever kiss a beautiful, golden princess—not ever become a debonair prince—not ever fall in love—not ever live happily ever after.

Angelina wept from her very soul, large droplets of sorrow, for the untimely fate of her small friend. As she wept, her heart's compassion reached out to the many creatures and many beings across the kingdom who were still patiently waiting, and some not so patiently waiting, for their own magical moment. The salty flow seemed unceasing, rushing away not only her own sweet sorrow but also the cherished illusions of halos and wings, fairy godmothers, and perfect eternal love. It was not until Angelina had cried her final tear and there were no more tears to be cried that she became completely still.

And so, in the quiet of the great woods, under the umbrella of a sun-dappled oak tree, there the poor lassie sat, empty of mind and empty of heart. For many moments, not a single thought passed her mind. She was aware of nothing more than the movement of her breath—traveling upwards, traveling downwards, traveling upwards, traveling downwards, and so on.

Now it happened, that within the place some might call the mind's eye, there appeared the sweet image of a delicate blossom, seemingly on the edge of bursting into bloom. In awe, Angelina watched as the flower opened, a single petal at a time until the beauty of the blossom filled her heart and radiated from her entire being. Then, it is told, a bright light flooded her senses and the lassie realized from somewhere deep inside herself, that this exquisite, enveloping sensation was the divine love she had been yearning for and searching for these past days, nights, weeks, months, and years.

In the stillness of that moment, Angelina suddenly knew without a doubt that she needn't be perfect to receive unconditional love—such love was her very birthright, simply for being a being. The riches within herself were available to any being or any creature willing to become still and listen to the silence, allowing the inner awareness to find that tender heart from which to love and be loved. And it was in the sharing of that love with others that one's heart would soar with the angels above.

Tisn't the end –

rather, a new beginning . . .

Appendix

Materials & Techniques

Additional Reading

Materials & Techniques

As you enter the unknown territory of the painting process, the materials and techniques you use during your explorations will establish a link between your thinking self and your intuitive self. To respond to the color from a dropper, or to spray a misting of water to encourage the flow of paint, is to become a part of the process. With practice and experimentation, you will discover various painting materials that seem to invite you to play and to explore, thereby allowing your creativity to express its deepest truth through the experience of painting.

Basic Materials

Plexiglas in various sizes (10"x12", 16"x20", 24"x32")

1/4" Plywood in various sizes (10"x12", 16"x20", 24"x32")

1/8" Illustration board (20"x30")

Watercolor paper in various sizes/weights (9"x12", 16"x20", 24"x30")
140 lb. cold press (rough surface)
140 lb. hot press (smooth surface)
300 lb. cold press (for layering and collaging artwork)

Masking tape

Liquid Watermedia
Drawing Inks (Common brands: FW, Higgins, Winsor & Newton)
Concentrated Water Colors (Luma, Dr. Ph. Martin's)

Watercolour pencils

Acrylic medium (gloss or matte finish)

Japanese-style hake brush

Materials & Techniques, cont.

Paint applicators (available through beauty supply stores)
    Several small plastic bottles with applicator tips
    Several small plastic spray bottles
    Droppers

An assortment of materials for texturing

Natural	Shells, stones, leaves, grasses, flower blossoms, feathers, evergreen needles, fossilized rock
Recyclable	Plastic dropcloth, plastic shower curtain with/without embossed pattern, plastic food wrap, cellophane
Fiber/Fabric	Lace, cheesecloth, gauze, burlap, needlepoint screening, open-weave fabrics
Paper	Tissue, Japanese rice, handmade

Paper towel

Acid-free 1/2" foam core boards (24"x30")

Lightweight plastic drop cloth, cut into various sizes

Preparation

Cover your worktable with a plastic drop cloth. If the thought of painting outdoors appeals to you, just remember that the weather (sun, rain, clouds) can have an effect on your painting, especially with regard to drying time.

Fill several small plastic bottles with individual colors of drawing ink or concentrated water color, attaching an applicator tip to the colors you plan to pour or a spray attachment to those you plan to mist.

When experimenting with a new technique or material(s), I usually begin with several small (8"x10") pieces of watercolor paper and/or illustration board which are taped to individual pieces of Plexiglas. Once I discover my own method of working with the technique/material(s) I will then increase the size of my artboard.

Materials & Techniques, cont.

Pouring Color

Prepare your painting surface by attaching a piece of watercolor paper or illustration board to a piece of Plexiglas with masking tape. Lightly brush the surface with water using a Japanese-style hake brush, letting the paper dry fully before applying color.

You can either rewet the surface by lightly spraying it with water or work on the dry surface, depending upon the effect you want to create. If the surface is wet, the poured or dripped color will produce soft edges and blended areas whereas paint applied to a dry surface will result in more distinct colors with harder edges.

After you squirt, spray, or drip a small amount of color onto the paper, place your fingers beneath the edges of the Plexiglas, and tilt the painting from side to side, letting gravity affect the flow of color. You can work with a single color at a time—or a few colors at once, letting them blend together. Continue to apply the colors, from light to dark, using only three or four colors. To direct the flow of paint, use a hake brush moistened with a small amount of water; continue tilting the board. At some point, step back from the table to view your work from a distance. Check to see if there are any areas that still need color or any spots that might be too dark and need additional water. Wait until you are prompted by your intuition before proceeding.

Once you feel that the composition of your painting is complete, cover the entire piece with lightweight plastic, letting the plastic fall where it may. Place a plywood board across the painting to establish contact between the plastic, paint, and paper; this will create a glossy sheen on your artwork. After twenty-four hours, remove the plywood and the plastic, revealing the expression of beauty that you created, in hand with nature.

Materials & Techniques, cont.

Creating Texture

By simply placing natural or manmade objects on top of wet color and letting the objects dry in place, you can develop form and texture within a painting. To begin, create a painting as described on the preceding page, keeping in mind that it will become the background design upon which you will explore the patterns of nature.

Once you are satisfied with the basic composition, place several objects directly into the color with the flattest side facing down. Then, tilting the board slightly, allow the color to flow. The weight of the objects will attract the paint, creating puddles around the items. At this point, if you want to add more color, use a spray bottle to do so, thereby preventing any shifting of the items.

When you sense that your artwork is complete, scrunch a large piece of plastic wrap in your hand, open it up, and arrange it loosely over the objects, attempting to cover the entire painting. Place items such as books or cans on top of the plastic to help insure contact between the various surfaces.

Wait at least twenty-four hours before checking to see if the painting is dry. The actual drying time will vary, depending upon the type and number of objects used. The texture and form that is created is determined by the object(s) used, the amount of color, and the degree of contact between paper, paint, and object. If a painting is "opened up" before it is dry, some of the texturing may be lost if the objects shift, so be sure to wait until the drying process is complete before removing the plastic cover and the texturing items. Your practice of patience will be rewarded with the gift of nature's unique imprint appearing within the context of your own inner landscape.

Materials & Techniques, cont.

Texturing with Nature

Begin collecting items from nature's playground that are intricately designed—leaves, flower blossoms, grasses, pine needles, bark, shells. Any natural item that is somewhat porous and has at least one side that is relatively flat will create texture. Natural items can be used and reused—simply spraying the piece of nature with water before placing it in the paint will bring out its natural design.

Texturing with Plastic Wrap

Place a large piece of plastic wrap across a painting that you just designed with color. Using the palm of your hand or your fingertips, manipulate the plastic wrap, creating patterns such as swirls or ridges. Wherever the plastic touches the wet paper, the color will be trapped and held. You can also add more paint by slipping a dropper filled with color under the edges of the plastic and releasing the color into the creases. The color will follow the shape of the material it touches and when dry, will permanently reveal that shape.

Texturing with Waxed Paper

A full sheet of waxed paper that is folded and unfolded, placed across a wet painting, and then left to dry, will produce a unique effect. Waxed paper can also be cut or torn into shapes and images that are placed directly in the ink or water color. After arranging several waxed shapes into a design, add more color if needed, cover the entire piece with a plastic drop cloth, and let the artwork dry overnight.

Upon removing the plastic and the waxed paper, you will discover that the textured areas now have a smooth and glossy finish that can be rubbed until it almost glows. If you spray a new color on the painting at this time—the waxed areas will not accept the color, while the unwaxed areas will—thus, the new color will highlight the textured forms.

Materials & Techniques, cont.

Texturing with Paper

Tissue paper, Japanese rice paper, and handmade paper can all be easily torn or cut into shapes and placed directly into wet ink to create forms with texture. Paper is the only material that needs to be removed from the painting surface <u>before</u> the painting is completely dry or the shapes may permanently stick. Once the painting is dry, the paper shapes can be glued onto the painting, thereby creating additional effects.

Texturing with Fibers

Cut a tube of cheesecloth or an old nylon stocking lengthwise and place it flat on a tabletop. After unhooking the top and bottom threads, begin pulling on the threads to make the material "run." Keep running the fibers until some sections are loose or open. The looser the material is from being pulled, the more interesting your design will be.

After dampening the material with water, lightly spray your painting surface with one or two colors, and then drape the fiber across the color in some design. Once you are satisfied with the placement of the fibers, spray additional color to add detail and depth. When you feel that your work is complete, cover it with plastic wrap and allow to dry for at least twenty-four hours. After removing the plastic wrap, you can either remove the fibers, revealing a realistic textural effect, or you can leave the fibers in place, exhibiting its true texture.

Texturing with Lace

Using lace to create texture and design is very easy, yet the results can be quite beautiful. Lightly mist a piece of lace with water and place it on a sheet of watercolor paper you just sprayed with color, cover the piece with plastic wrap, and let it dry overnight. Upon removing the plastic and the lace, an image of its intricate design will be revealed. This truly is a gift of the angels!

Creating with Collage

My hope is that you will save all of the paintings you create as you explore the painting process, even the ones that don't seem to say anything. A painting that may appear unresolved or incomplete can be reborn at another time by using it as a background piece, or cutting and tearing it into collage material. When you are uncertain about whether a painting is finished or not, place the artwork in a location where you can see it and let your intuition guide you. It may need just a bit more color or texture; or you might collage a section of another painting onto the unfinished one, thereby creating an image that feels complete; or the unfinished piece could become the background design for a new painting. By staying in touch with your inner wisdom, you will gradually know what to do.

When collaging large pieces of two or three complementary paintings, play with the images before deciding upon a final composition. Using a piece of watercolor paper (300 lb.) or illustration board as the background, brush the surface with water and then apply color, if desired. Once the background is completely dry, attach the torn pieces according to your design, using a gloss medium as glue.

A collage can also be created using a variety of pieces and shapes that are unrelated. Tear or cut the pieces into smaller pieces, coloring the edges with watercolour pencils. Play with the various pieces on a sheet of foam core board, arranging them in various patterns until you find the one that feels right. Using an acrylic gloss medium, attach the collage materials to the foam board, leaving the piece uncovered to dry.

Once your collage materials are permanently in place, you can apply a coat of glossy medium in order to create a smooth finish. After brushing the medium across the surface, let the painting dry for at least thirty minutes. The expression you have created will reflect the true essence of nature's grace—beauty is anywhere and everywhere, if one can be still to see.

Additional Reading

Meditation, Spirituality

Bender, Sue. Everyday Sacred. HarperSanFrancisco, HarperCollins: New York, 1995.

Chodron, Pema. When Things Fall Apart. Shambala Publications: Boston and London, 1997.

Kornfield, Jack. A Path With Heart. Bantam Books: New York, 1993.

Muller, Wayne. Legacy of the Heart. Simon and Schuster: New York, 1992.

Obson, Diane K., Editor. A Joseph Campbell Companion. Harper Collins: New York, 1991.

Remen, Rachel Naomi, M.D. Kitchen Table Wisdom. Riverhead Books: New York, 1996.

Creativity, Writing

Bennett, Hal Zina. Write From the Heart. New World Library: Novato, CA, 1995, 2000.

Cameron, Julia. The Artist's Way. Jeremy P. Tarcher/Perigee: New York, 1992.

Goldberg, Natalie. Wild Mind. Bantam Books: New York, 1990.

Art

Carbonetti, Jeanne. The Tao of Watercolor. Watson-Guptill: New York, 1998.

Masterfield, Maxine. In Harmony With Nature. Watson-Guptill: New York, 1990.

Masterfield, Maxine. Painting the Spirit of Nature. Watson-Guptill: New York, 1984.